EXPLORING SCIENCE

CHEMICAL CHANGE

FROM FIREWORKS TO RUST

BY DARLENE R. STILLE

Content Adviser: Elie Abushanab, Emeritus Professor
of Organic Chemistry, University of Rhode Island

Science Adviser: Terrence E. Young Jr., M.Ed., M.L.S.,
Jefferson Parish (Louisiana) Public School System

Reading Adviser: Susan Kesselring, M.A., Literacy Educator,
Rosemount-Apple Valley-Eagan (Minnesota) School District

COMPASS POINT BOOKS · MINNEAPOLIS, MINNESOTA

Compass Point Books • 3109 West 50th Street, #115 • Minneapolis, MN 55410

Visit Compass Point Books on the Internet at *www.compasspointbooks.com*
or e-mail your request to *custserv@compasspointbooks.com*

Photographs ©: Corbis, cover, 32–33; Time Life Pictures/Mansell/Getty Images, 4; OneBlueShoe, 5; ML Sinibaldi/Corbis, 6; Digital Vision, 7; Mary Evans Picture Library, 9; Ed Reschke/Peter Arnold, Inc., 10; Leonard Lessin/Peter Arnold, Inc., 11; Stephen J. Boitano/Getty Images, 12; Scott Bauer/USDA/ARS, 13; Mimmo Jodice/Corbis, 15; Lester V. Bergman/Corbis, 18; Hulton Archive/Getty Images, 19, 42; The Granger Collection, New York, 20; Martin Harvey/Corbis, 21; Bruce Dale/National Geographic/Getty Images, 24; Jan-Peter Lahall/Peter Arnold, Inc., 26–27; Doug Sokell/Tom Stack & Associates, 30; North Wind Picture Archives, 31; Carl A. Stimac/The Image Finders, 34; Creatas, 37; Science Museum, Science & Society Picture Library, 38; Roger Ball/Corbis, 39; Andrew Brown; Ecoscene/Corbis, 40; Alen MacWeeney/Corbis, 41; Dr. John D. Cunningham/Visuals Unlimited, 43; Richard Hamilton Smith, 46.

Editor: Nadia Higgins
Designer/Page Production: The Design Lab
Lead Designer: Jaime Martins
Photo Researcher: Marcie C. Spence
Cartographer: XNR Productions, Inc.
Illustrator: Farhana Hossain
Educational Consultant: Diane Smolinski

Managing Editor: Catherine Neitge
Creative Director: Keith Griffin
Editorial Director: Carol Jones

Library of Congress Cataloging-in-Publication Data
Stille, Darlene R.
  Chemical change : from fireworks to rust / by Darlene R. Stille.
    p. cm. — (Exploring science)
  Includes bibliographical references and index.
  ISBN 0-7565-1256-5
  1. Chemical reactions—Juvenile literature. 2. Chemistry—History—Juvenile literature. 3. Matter—Properties—Juvenile literature. I. Title. II. Exploring science (Minneapolis, Minn.)
  QD501.S853 2006
  541'.39—dc22   2005002475

About the Author

Darlene R. Stille is a science writer and author of more than 70 books for young people. When she was in high school, she fell in love with science. While attending the University of Illinois, she discovered that she also loved writing. She was fortunate enough to find a career as an editor and writer that allowed her to combine both of her interests. Darlene Stille now lives and writes in Michigan.

TABLE OF CONTENTS

CHAPTER ONE

What Is Chemical Change?

A FLAME DANCES on the tip of a candle. A burning log crackles in the fireplace. Fire changes the wick of a candle and the wood of the log into smoke and ashes.

Ancient people learned to use the power of fire. They learned that fire could give off heat to keep them warm and cook their food. The flames of oil lamps or torches lighted their homes in the dark of night. To them, fire was mysterious and sacred.

Early scientists studied fire. By the 1700s, they understood that fire is part of something much larger—fire is one of the forces that brings about chemical change.

Prehistoric human beings, or Neanderthals, were using fire more than 35,000 years ago in Europe and Asia.

A WORLD OF CHANGE

Matter is all the material in the world—anything that takes up space, including trees, rocks, and even air. The sun, moon, stars, plants, animals, and you are made of matter, too. All matter is constantly changing, though.

Matter can change in one of two ways, physically or chemically. A physical change is generally much less complete and permanent than a chemical change. Physical change just makes matter look or feel different.

Steam rising from water is an example of a physical, as opposed to chemical, change.

Water freezing into ice or boiling into steam are examples of physical change. Ice, water, and steam may appear to be very different from one another. They are, however, just different forms of water. The water itself does not change into something new. Chopping wood, mixing oil and vinegar, or sculpting clay are other examples of physical change.

A stand of charred trees after a forest fire at Yosemite National Park, California, shows how fire creates chemical changes. Unlike many physical changes, chemical changes are not easily reversed.

Changes in matter that *do* create new substances are chemical changes. When wood burns, it changes into matter with different chemical properties—gray, flaky ashes and wispy smoke. This is just one of thousands of chemical changes that occur around us.

DID YOU KNOW?

A LIGHTNING CHANGE

When a lightning bolt flashes during a thunderstorm, it causes a chemical change in the air around it. Nitrogen and oxygen, two gases in the air, combine to make new gases called nitrogen oxides. Raindrops carrying the nitrogen oxides fall to the earth. In the soil, another chemical change turns the nitrogen oxides into fertilizer that helps plants grow.

Earth, Air, Fire, and Water

For many thousands of years, people used fire to create chemical change. They burned wood for heat. They burned oil for light. They melted rocks called ore to make iron and other metals. They had no idea that they were causing chemical change.

The ancient Greeks began to wonder how and why things in the world changed. A Greek philosopher in the 400s B.C. named Empedocles came up with the idea of elements. His elements were not like the chemical elements we know about in modern science. Today, we know that there are 94 chemical elements found in nature, such as gold or oxygen, and that these cannot be broken down into other substances. Empedocles thought there were only four elements—earth, air, fire, and water.

In the 300s B.C., a famous Greek philosopher named Aristotle said that any of these four elements could be changed into another element by adding heat or moisture. Adding heat to water, for example, would change the water into air. For almost 2,000 years, people believed the ideas of the ancient Greeks about how new substances were made. Today, we know that chemical reactions between chemical elements make new substances.

In the 1600s, people began to do more careful experiments. An Irish scientist named Robert Boyle was the first real chemist. He believed that all matter was made of atoms—the tiniest, most

basic building blocks of elements. He did careful experiments on gases and other substances. He proved that earth, air, fire, and water were not true elements.

The Greek philosopher Empedocles [495?–435? B.C.] said that love was the force that caused Earth's four elements to combine. Strife [fighting] made them break apart.

THE POWER OF CHEMICAL CHANGE

Chemical changes keep plants and animals alive. Green plants use energy from the sun to make food through a chemical process called photosynthesis. In digestion, chemical changes in the body break down food and release its energy.

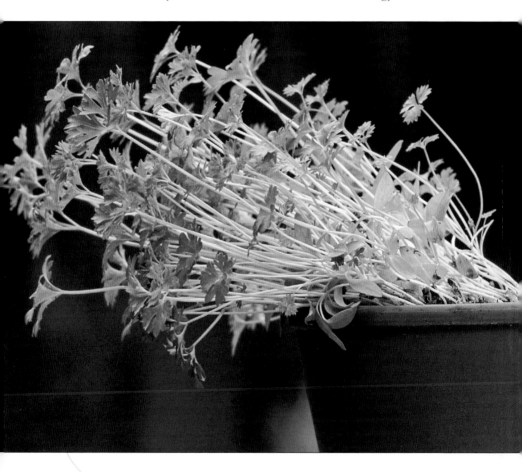

A parsley plant bends toward light. Through photosynthesis, the plant converts sunlight, water, and carbon dioxide (a gas in the air) into food.

Chemical changes are also necessary for many of life's pleasures and conveniences. As a cake bakes in an oven, the flour, eggs, and butter that made up the batter change. As gasoline burns, it releases energy that powers a car. From laundry detergents and aspirin to nylon stockings and rain boots, products researched and developed by chemists fill our cabinets and closets.

Other chemical changes, however, can be a nuisance, or worse. Shiny silver will tarnish, or turn black, over time. The steel handle on a car door will rust and stick. Much more serious are chemical changes in the cells in our bodies that lead to diseases. Pollutants in the environment cause harmful chemical changes in plants, wildlife, and people.

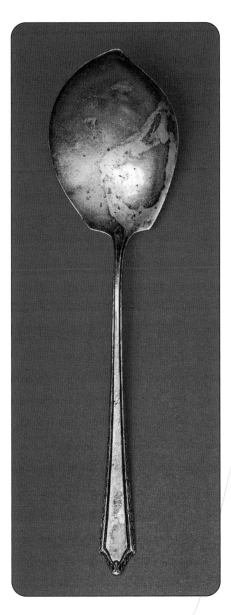

As silver combines with oxygen in the air, it tarnishes, or turns black.

Scientists harness the power of chemical change as they research and create new medicines and products. Scientists also look for ways to prevent or slow the chemical changes in our bodies that cause disease. They have learned, for example, that substances called antioxidants, such as vitamin C, can help prevent some of these harmful chemical changes.

Understanding how chemical changes come about and how they can work for good or cause harm is important. This information can help lawmakers and ordinary citizens make informed decisions about issues crucial to our well-being. What foods are most healthy and which should be avoided? What medicines should we take? How can we protect the environment? Understanding chemical change is a key part of finding answers to these questions.

Scientists for public health agencies appear before the U.S. House of Representatives in October 2004. The scientists were informing lawmakers about a severe shortage of flu shots that year.

The Secrets of Life

Do you want to unlock the deepest secrets of life? Then you might want to become a biochemist. Biochemistry is part biology, part chemistry. Biochemists try to understand how plants

A biochemist (left) and a physical scientist use a special machine to measure a form of copper in the blood.

and animal bodies work by studying the chemical changes that take place inside them.

Biochemists tackle questions such as, How do green plants make their own food? Photosynthesis is the answer. Biochemists learned that an amazing chemical process between water and carbon dioxide from the air occurs inside plants. In the presence of sunlight, the water and carbon dioxide become sugar. Plants use the sugar as food.

Why do children inherit eye color, hair color, and all other traits from their parents? Biochemists and other scientists found the answer to this and many other questions in DNA, the master molecule of life. DNA not only passes along inherited traits, but also controls everything that goes on in all plants and animals. For every question biochemists answered about DNA, several more questions came up.

The study of changes in DNA has led to the creation of new drugs. It also has led doctors to understand more about inherited diseases. And the work on DNA is really just getting started. Biochemists hope to use their knowledge about DNA's biochemical changes to cure or treat many deadly diseases— including many kinds of cancers.

CHAPTER TWO

Atoms and Molecules: Building Blocks of Chemical Change

ALL CHEMICALS AND chemical change begin with atoms and elements. In nature, there are 94 distinct kinds of atoms. We can think of nature's atoms as being like a set of building blocks that join together to make all the things in the universe. The blocks come in 94 different colors and patterns. Some blocks are red, for example, while others are blue, green, or yellow. Some have stripes and others have dots. Each unique block is a different kind of atom.

Each kind of atom makes up a different chemical element, such as gold or carbon. These are substances that cannot be broken down through chemical change. For example, water is *not*

Gold, one of nature's 94 chemical elements, does not tarnish and is easy to bend and shape. This pure gold charm, from the ancient city of Pompeii in Italy, is more than 2,000 years old.

an element, so it can be broken down into the simpler substances oxygen and hydrogen. But oxygen and hydrogen cannot be broken down into other substances. They are elements.

Each atom is incredibly tiny. Millions of them would fit inside the period at the end of this sentence. These atoms join together to make slightly larger units of matter called molecules. When the atoms separate from each other, the molecules break apart. As long as two or more different kinds of atoms are involved, both actions—molecules forming and molecules breaking apart—create chemical change.

CHEMICAL COMPOUNDS

For example, chemical change makes water from oxygen and hydrogen atoms. Oxygen and hydrogen are normally gases. Oxygen is the gas we breathe in order to live. Hydrogen is a gas that burns easily.

Under the right conditions, putting two hydrogen atoms and one oxygen atom together makes one molecule of water. Water is not like oxygen or hydrogen alone. Water is a completely different substance—a slippery, wet liquid—with a new chemical makeup. It is a chemical compound.

Since a water molecule just has three atoms from two elements, it is a simple chemical compound. Some compounds are much more complex. Vitamins are made of huge molecules with as many as 50 atoms.

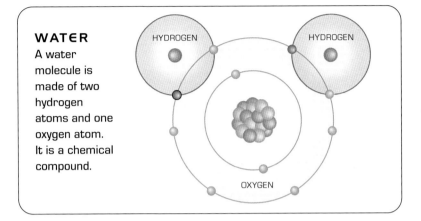

WATER
A water molecule is made of two hydrogen atoms and one oxygen atom. It is a chemical compound.

HYDROGEN

HYDROGEN

OXYGEN

Sometimes, atoms of the same kind, or element, link up to form a molecule. For example, oxygen molecules in the air are made up of just two oxygen atoms. This is not a chemical change, since no new substance is created. The oxygen molecule is still pure oxygen.

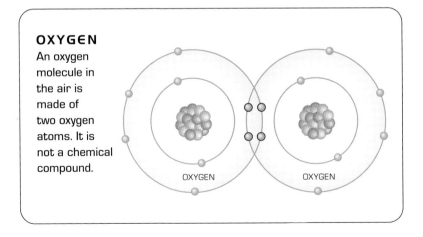

OXYGEN
An oxygen molecule in the air is made of two oxygen atoms. It is not a chemical compound.

OXYGEN

OXYGEN

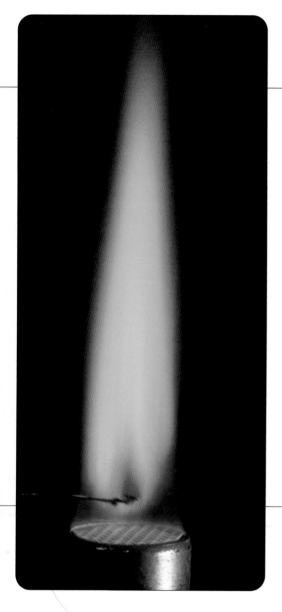

DID YOU KNOW?

COLORFUL FLAMES

Chemists sometimes use the flame test to figure out what elements are in a chemical compound. They put some of the compound on a platinum wire and hold the wire in a flame. They watch to see what color the flame turns. Calcium makes the flame turn orangey red. Copper makes the flame turn emerald green (left). Sodium burns with a yellow flame, and potassium gives off a purple flame.

The Periodic Table

The idea that each element was made of different atoms came from the English chemist John Dalton in the early 1800s. Eventually, chemists learned that there are 94 naturally occurring chemical elements and 16 or even more elements that scientists made in laboratories. Scientists gave each element a one- or two-letter symbol. For example, O stood for oxygen, C stood for carbon, Fe for iron, and Pb for lead. They found that chemical changes could create millions of chemical compounds. How could chemists keep track of all this information?

A Russian scientist named Dmitri Mendeleev asked the same question. In 1869, he created a way of organizing elements called the Periodic Table. Mendeleev wrote down everything that was known about the chemical elements

Russian scientist Dmitri Ivanovich Mendeleev (1834–1907) revolutionized the study of chemistry.

ПЕРИОДИЧЕСКАЯ СИСТЕМА ЭЛЕМЕНТОВ

ПЕРИОДЫ	РЯДЫ	ГРУППЫ ЭЛЕМЕНТОВ									
		I	II	III	IV	V	VI	VII	VIII		0
1	I	H ^{1} 1,008									He ^{2} 4,003
2	II	Li ^{3} 6,940	Be ^{4} 9,02	^{5} B 10,82	^{6} C 12,010	^{7} N 14,008	^{8} O 16,000	^{9} F 19,00			Ne ^{10} 20,183
3	III	Na ^{11} 22,997	Mg ^{12} 24,32	^{13} Al 26,97	^{14} Si 28,06	^{15} P 30,98	^{16} S 32,06	^{17} Cl 35,457			Ar ^{18} 39,944
4	IV	K ^{19} 39,096	Ca ^{20} 40,08	Sc ^{21} 45,10	Ti ^{22} 47,90	V ^{23} 50,95	Cr ^{24} 52,01	Mn ^{25} 54,93	Fe ^{26} 55,85	Co ^{27} 58,94	Ni ^{28} 58,69	
	V	^{29} Cu 63,57	^{30} Zn 65,38	^{31} Ga 69,72	^{32} Ge 72,60	^{33} As 74,91	^{34} Se 78,96	^{35} Br 79,916			Kr ^{36} 83,7
5	VI	Rb ^{37} 85,48	Sr ^{38} 87,63	Y ^{39} 88,92	Zr ^{40} 91,22	Nb ^{41} 92,91	Mo ^{42} 95,95	Ma ^{43} —	Ru ^{44} 101,7	Rh ^{45} 102,91	Pd ^{46} 106,7	
	VII	^{47} Ag 107,88	^{48} Cd 112,41	^{49} In 114,76	^{50} Sn 118,70	^{51} Sb 121,76	^{52} Te 127,61	^{53} J 126,92			Xe ^{54} 131,3
6	VIII	Cs ^{55} 132,91	Ba ^{56} 137,36	La ^{57} 138,92	Hf ^{72} 178,6	Ta ^{73} 180,88	W ^{74} 183,92	Re ^{75} 186,31	Os ^{76} 190,2	Ir ^{77} 193,1	Pt ^{78} 195,23	
	IX	^{79} Au 197,2	^{80} Hg 200,61	^{81} Tl 204,39	^{82} Pb 207,21	^{83} Bi 209,00	^{84} Po 210	^{85} —			Rn ^{86} 222
7	X	—	Ra ^{88} 226,05	Ac ^{89} 227	Th ^{90} 232,12	Pa ^{91} 231	U ^{92} 238,07				

★ ЛАНТАНИДЫ 58–71

Ce ^{58} 140,13	Pr ^{59} 140,92	Nd ^{60} 144,27	^{61} —	Sm ^{62} 150,43	Eu ^{63} 152,0	Gd ^{64} 156,9
Tb ^{65} 159,2	Dy ^{66} 162,46	Ho ^{67} 164,94	Er ^{68} 167,2	Tu ^{69} 169,4	Yb ^{70} 173,04	Cp ^{71} 174,99

and their properties. He saw that the elements could best be sorted by how many protons each atom had. Protons are tiny particles inside the atom's nucleus, or center. He called the number of protons the atomic number.

Sorted this way, the elements formed groups such as metals and nonmetals. Using the Periodic Table, chemists could easily identify an element's chemical properties, such as how readily it would combine with other elements.

Mendeleev left some spaces blank for unknown elements in his original Periodic Table. Using his table, he predicted the properties of three of the missing elements. When these elements were later discovered, they fit his descriptions.

COMPOUNDS OR MIXTURES?

Chemical compounds aren't to be confused with mixtures. Like chemical compounds, mixtures are made of more than one element. But mixtures are the result of physical, rather than chemical, change. In mixtures, atoms may move closer to one another, but the atoms do not join together to make new substances.

Air is not a chemical compound. It is a mixture of oxygen, nitrogen, carbon dioxide, and other gases. Bronze is a metal mixture, called an alloy, of the elements of copper and tin.

Compounds always have the same "recipe," or proportions, of elements. Water always has one oxygen atom for every two hydrogen atoms. Mixtures can have differing amounts of substances. Air at high elevations such as mountaintops has less oxygen than it does at sea level.

This door knocker on a traditional Moroccan restaurant is made of brass, a mixture—as opposed to a chemical compound—of copper and zinc. Because it is stronger than pure copper, brass serves many purposes and has been in use for more than 2,000 years.

CHAPTER THREE

Chemical Compounds: How Atoms Join

TINY ATOMS ARE made of even tinier parts. The center of the atom is called the nucleus. Inside the nucleus are tiny particles called protons and neutrons. The nucleus is surrounded by electrons. The number of electrons in an atom is always equal to the number of protons. What makes each element different is the number of protons and electrons in the atom.

Imagine an atom as a tiny solar system. Instead of the sun, the atom's nucleus is at the center of this solar system. Instead of planets, electrons orbit the center of the atom. This picture of the atom was first described by Danish physicist Neils Bohr in 1913. This picture, or model, can help us picture how atoms bond with one another.

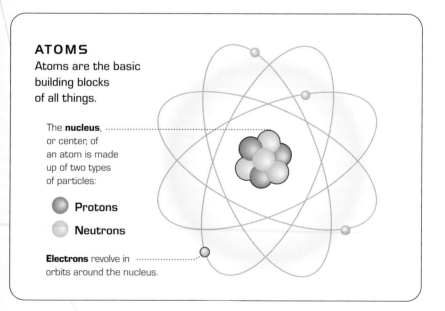

ATOMS
Atoms are the basic building blocks of all things.

The **nucleus**, or center, of an atom is made up of two types of particles:

● Protons

○ Neutrons

Electrons revolve in orbits around the nucleus.

HEAVY AND LIGHT

The atoms of each element have different weights. Hydrogen is the lightest and simplest element. It has just one proton in its nucleus and one electron orbiting around the nucleus. Plutonium is the largest natural element and is more than 200 times heavier than hydrogen. It has 94 protons, 150 neutrons, and 94 electrons.

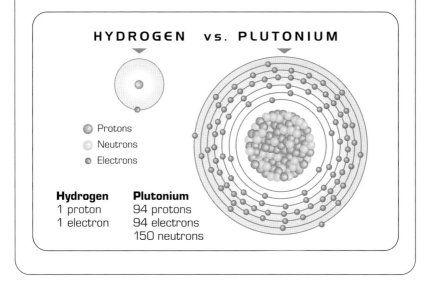

HYDROGEN vs. PLUTONIUM

- Protons
- Neutrons
- Electrons

Hydrogen
1 proton
1 electron

Plutonium
94 protons
94 electrons
150 neutrons

Atoms use their electrons to form a chemical bond. The atoms give away or share their electrons with one another. When different kinds of atoms share electrons, chemical changes take place, and chemical changes create new substances.

Not every kind of atom can join with every other kind of atom to make compounds. You can think of atoms as being a little like puzzle pieces. Only the pieces with the right shapes will fit together. The gases helium and hydrogen cannot join together. The metals iron and aluminum cannot make a compound, either.

Atoms can use their electrons to form bonds because some atoms can give up electrons while other atoms can accept more electrons. In other words, some atoms "want" to lose electrons, while others "want" to gain electrons.

Table salt provides an example of how atoms lose and gain electrons. Table salt is made of sodium and chlorine. As elements, sodium is a silvery metal while chlorine is a poisonous gas. But together, they make the ordinary salt we put on our food.

How do they do this? Atoms of sodium can give up electrons, and chlorine atoms can accept electrons. So chlorine takes some of

A close-up of a stream of table salt shows its clear, cube-shaped crystals. Salt is a common chemical compound that, in moderation, is crucial to good health.

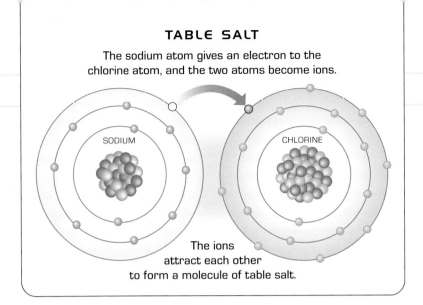

TABLE SALT

The sodium atom gives an electron to the chlorine atom, and the two atoms become ions.

SODIUM

CHLORINE

The ions attract each other to form a molecule of table salt.

sodium's electrons. Once an atom loses or gains electrons, it is called an ion. The sodium and chlorine ions attract each other to make a compound called sodium chloride, or table salt.

CHEMICAL SYMBOLS

Chemists use symbols to show how elements combine to make compounds. Each element has a symbol. The symbol for sodium is Na. The symbol for chlorine is Cl.

To show that two elements can combine, chemists use a plus sign (+).

To show what compound the combination of two elements makes, chemists use an arrow (−>), which stands for "yields."

When these symbols are put together, they make a chemical equation. The chemical equation for table salt is:

Na + Cl −> NaCl

That means, one sodium atom combined with one chlorine atom makes one molecule of sodium chloride.

Two Main Branches of Chemistry

Chemical compounds are grouped into two main types—organic and inorganic. Organic compounds are mainly found in living things. They also come from things that were once alive. Inorganic compounds are found mainly in nonliving things, such as rocks and minerals.

Organic chemicals are compounds that contain atoms of the element carbon. There are millions of different organic compounds—far more than inorganic ones. Petroleum, coal, and other fossil fuels are made of organic compounds called hydrocarbons. They are molecules of carbon and hydrogen atoms joined together. Hydrocarbons formed from the remains of animals and plants that died millions of years ago. Chemical companies use hydrocarbons to make many products, from gasoline

to plastics. Chemists can also make organic compounds in the laboratory.

Inorganic compounds are found in all nonliving things. Inorganic chemicals are chemical compounds that do not contain carbon atoms. They also include those rocks and minerals, such as diamond and graphite, which *only* contain atoms of carbon. The 94 basic chemical elements, including carbon, are also inorganic chemicals. Aluminum cans, iron frying pans, and certain kinds of drugs are made from inorganic elements and compounds. Some inorganic molecules, such as water and salt, are also abundant in living things.

Like substances such as sugar and alcohol, coal is made of organic chemicals. Most of Earth's coal formed from ferns and treelike plants that grew in swamps more than 286 million years ago.

CHAPTER FOUR

Fast and Slow "Burns"

SOME CHEMICAL CHANGES happen in seconds, while others can take months or even years. Scientists have learned that oxygen takes part in certain fast and slow chemical changes.

OXYGEN AND COMBUSTION

Oxygen often plays a role in a fast change called combustion, which is a chemical change that gives off heat and light. Striking a match causes combustion. A spark from friction on the match tip causes a flame to burn at the end of the match. Holding the match to a piece of paper causes the paper to burn.

In combustion, oxygen in the air rapidly joins, or combines, with a fuel. The fuel can be a solid, such as paper or wood, or a liquid, such as charcoal lighter fluid. It can also be a gas, such as the natural gas that comes out of a burner on a stove.

In order to burn, a solid or liquid fuel must first be changed to a gas. This change requires heat. The heat from a match or other flame "loosens" molecules on the surface of wood, paper, or lighter fluid. The freed molecules turn into a gas that combines with oxygen in the air.

Paper, wood, and other materials must be heated to a certain temperature for molecules on their surface to turn into a gas. This temperature

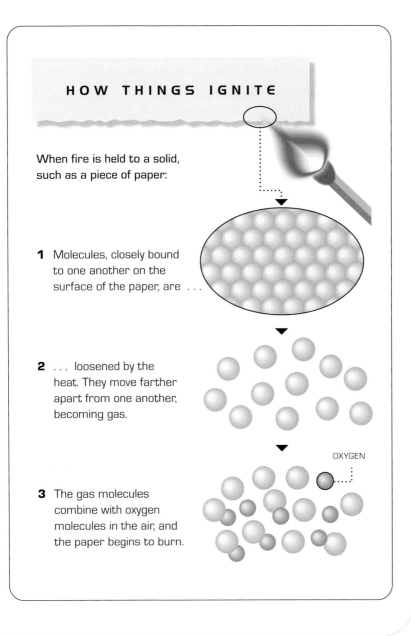

HOW THINGS IGNITE

When fire is held to a solid, such as a piece of paper:

1 Molecules, closely bound to one another on the surface of the paper, are . . .

2 . . . loosened by the heat. They move farther apart from one another, becoming gas.

OXYGEN

3 The gas molecules combine with oxygen molecules in the air, and the paper begins to burn.

is called the ignition temperature. At this temperature, gas molecules freed from the fuel's surface combine with oxygen in the air. The fuel ignites, or begins to burn.

Solids usually have higher ignition temperatures than liquids or gases. Wood begins to burn when its temperature reaches between 572 and 689 degrees Fahrenheit (300 to 365 degrees Celsius). Gasoline's ignition temperature is much lower at -36 degrees Fahrenheit (-38 degrees C), which explains why a car can still start up on a cold day.

DID YOU KNOW?

NOTHING LOST

When a fuel such as wood burns, it seems as if some of its matter "disappears." The ashy remains weigh much less than the original log. However, scientists have proved that, except in extreme situations, matter is never destroyed. Part of the log turned to gas that floated away. The weight of the ashes plus all the other gaseous by-products of the fire would equal the original weight of the log.

Oxygen, Not Phlogiston

The question of why things burn led to many discoveries in chemistry. In the 1700s, a German scientist named Georg Ernst Stahl said that anything that can burn contains an odorless, colorless, and weightless substance called phlogiston. Chemists spent a lot of time looking for phlogiston. In doing so, they developed ways to study gases and discovered carbon dioxide, hydrogen, and oxygen.

In 1772, a French chemist named Antoine Lavoisier solved the mystery of why things burn. He did careful experiments by burning things and weighing them before and afterward. He also trapped and weighed the air that the substances burned in. After burning, the air weighed less, but the burned substances weighed more. He concluded that burning removed a gas from the air. He found that the gas oxygen combined with substances when they burned. So there really was no such thing as phlogiston.

French chemist Antoine Lavoisier (1743–1794) is considered to be the founder of modern chemistry.

EXPLOSION: VERY FAST CHEMICAL CHANGE

A rocket zooms up into the air and—boom! The end of the rocket sends out showers of hot sparks that make beautiful fireworks in the sky. The fireworks are caused by a very fast chemical change called an explosion.

The main material in fireworks is a chemical compound called gunpowder. The gunpowder is packed into a cardboard tube or other container. The heat from a lighted fuse causes the gunpowder to rapidly combine with oxygen in the air. This sudden chemical change gives off a lot of different kinds of gases. Because of special chemicals that have been added to the gunpowder, each kind of gas has its own dazzling color. The fireworks we see are burning gases exploding out of the container.

RUSTING: VERY SLOW CHANGE

An old car may sit outside in rain and snow for months or even years. Brownish-red patches begin to form on the car and spread over larger and larger areas. The rust seems to "eat"

Fireworks offer a spectacular example of combustion, a chemical reaction that gives off light and heat.

the car body away as the metal turns to powder. This rust comes from slow chemical changes in steel and other metals that contain iron.

In dampness, iron atoms in metal combine with oxygen atoms that have dissolved in the water droplets. The iron and oxygen form a chemical compound called iron oxide. Iron oxide is the chemical name for rust. Rust is not like iron metal, nor is it like oxygen gas. Rust is a new substance made by chemical change. This chemical change is a lot like the change that happens when wood or paper joins with oxygen and burns. Rusting is like a very slow burn.

Rust can damage a truck beyond repair. If caught in time, however, rust can be scrubbed off or dissolved by acids.

In rusting, the iron atoms give up electrons and join with oxygen atoms. This is called an oxidation reaction. Oxidation is also involved in the way our bodies use food to produce energy.

HOW THE BODY BURNS FOOD

Milk, vegetables, fruits, and all the other things we eat are made of chemical compounds. Our bodies "burn" these foods for energy. Two French chemists, Antoine Lavoisier and Pierre Simon Laplace, discovered in the 1700s that the body uses oxygen to help burn food. Since then, scientists have learned much more about this process.

Digestion starts in the mouth as watery saliva begins to break down food. Acids in the stomach continue the chemical breakdown of food into sugars and other simpler compounds. Molecules of these compounds go from the stomach into the

---

DID YOU KNOW?

WARM TO THE TOUCH

The body doesn't really "burn" food. However, the process of digestion does create heat. Normal body temperature is 98.6 degrees Fahrenheit (37 degrees C). This is the result of chemical changes taking place as the body breaks down food.

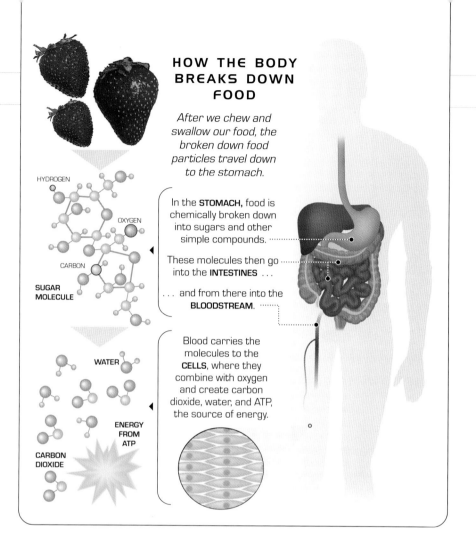

HOW THE BODY BREAKS DOWN FOOD

After we chew and swallow our food, the broken down food particles travel down to the stomach.

HYDROGEN

OXYGEN

CARBON

SUGAR MOLECULE

In the **STOMACH,** food is chemically broken down into sugars and other simple compounds.

These molecules then go into the **INTESTINES** . . .

. . . and from there into the **BLOODSTREAM.**

WATER

ENERGY FROM ATP

CARBON DIOXIDE

Blood carries the molecules to the **CELLS,** where they combine with oxygen and create carbon dioxide, water, and ATP, the source of energy.

intestines and from there into the bloodstream. The blood carries these molecules to the cells of the body.

In the cells, the food molecules combine with oxygen. The chemical reactions involved create carbon dioxide, water, and a chemical substance call ATP (adenosine triphosphate). ATP is the chemical substance that delivers energy to muscles and other cells.

EXERCISE AND ENERGY

Running, swimming, bicycling, and jogging are good forms of aerobic exercise. *Aerobic* means "with oxygen." Aerobic exercise speeds up certain chemical changes inside the body.

Aerobic exercise makes the lungs work harder to breathe in more air and, therefore, more oxygen. It also makes blood vessels better able to carry oxygen from the lungs to other parts of the body. Regular aerobic exercise increases the body's ability to use oxygen efficiently. The efficient use of oxygen helps body cells produce more ATP. The more ATP produced, the less likely a person is to feel tired during the day.

Because it uses all major muscle groups, swimming is one of the most intense forms of aerobic activity.

CHAPTER FIVE

Products from Chemical Change

THE MODERN CHEMICAL INDUSTRY began in Europe with simple products in the 1700s, such as soaps and acids. The first major chemical products were synthetic, or artificially made, dyes. The chemical dye industry came into being soon after English chemist William H. Perkin made the first synthetic dye, a pale purple called mauve, in 1856. Before then, people made dyes from bark, berries, and other natural resources. By the early 1900s, Germany had the world's largest dye industry, which employed many chemists.

Today, companies use chemical change to make all kinds of products, from dyes and detergents to medicines that treat and cure diseases. They make chemical fertilizers for growing better crops and chemical pesticides for killing insects and weeds.

This silk dress from 1862 was colored mauve using synthetic dye invented by William H. Perkin.

THE RISE OF PLASTICS

Today, plastics are one of the biggest chemical industries. Plastics have thousands of uses and come in a variety of forms. Companies make plastics that bend like string or are as strong as steel. Some companies make plastics for wrapping foods, weaving into clothes, or even for making car parts. It is hard to imagine life without plastics. A quick look around shows how

The word *plastics* comes from the Greek word *plastikos*, which means "able to be shaped." At this factory, plastic is stretched into thin sheets for wrapping food.

many objects in our everyday lives are made with plastic—
pens, computers, cups, eyeglasses, and shoes.

The invention of plastic was prompted by the game of bil-
liards, or pool, which was a popular game as early as the 1400s.
The little billiard balls were made of ivory from the tusks and teeth
of elephants, walruses, and whales. In the late 1800s, ivory became
scarce, and an American printer named John W. Hyatt invented a
new material to replace ivory. In his laboratory, he chemically
altered cellulose, a material in cotton, to create a hard material
called celluloid.

Versatile plastic has thousands of uses in industry as well as agriculture. Huge
sheets of plastic cover entire crops in Spain, protecting the plants from frost.

In 1909, American chemist Leo Baekeland patented a new material called Bakelite, the first real plastic. It was hard and tough and useful for making many products, from telephones to pot handles.

By studying Bakelite in their laboratories, chemists learned a lot about the kind of molecules that make up a plastic. Soon chemists learned to make other plastics such as acrylics, nylon, and polyesters. Plastics have replaced many materials such as metals, woods, and natural fabrics. Celluloid is still used to make ping-pong balls.

These desk clocks, dice, and lighters were made from Bakelite in the early 1900s. Leo Baekeland invented the early form of plastic during an attempt to invent another product—but the results were anything but a failure.

Early Inventors

From the early days of Christianity through the 1600s, a group of people called alchemists laid the foundations of chemistry. Alchemists wanted to change lead and other metals into pure gold. They also wanted to find a substance that would cure all sickness.

Alchemists also did experiments with mercury, salt, and sulfur. They invented many tools used by later chemists such as bottles and beakers. They built ovens for heating solids and boiling liquids and invented scales for weighing powders. The alchemists also created many substances, such as acids and alcohols. Some of their experiments were very dangerous. They made chemicals that exploded or that turned out to be deadly poisons. They never did succeed in changing one element into another, but they paved the way for other scientists.

An alchemist from the 1600s tends to an experiment in the hope of creating gold.

WATER POLLUTION FROM CHEMICAL CHANGES

Chemicals made from chemical changes are very useful to daily life, but there is a downside. Some chemicals can cause serious environmental pollution. Many factories, oil refineries, and laboratories produce hazardous waste chemicals, such as poisons and explosives. Paint factories, for example, once created hazardous chemicals called PCBs (polychlorinated biphenyls) that can cause liver damage. Chemical fertilizers and pesticides that are washed off fields by rain can also run into streams and lakes and pollute water. Such hazardous wastes dumped into lakes and rivers can kill fish and other wildlife and endanger people's health.

ACID RAIN

The chemicals sulfur dioxide and nitrogen oxide cause a type of pollution called acid rain. Smoke from tall chimneys on factories and power plants contains these chemical compounds. The compounds join with water vapor in the air and change into powerful acids. The acids make polluted rain, snow, or fog that soaks into the ground and into lakes and rivers, killing fish, plants, and wildlife.

A statue in Europe has been eaten away by acid rain.

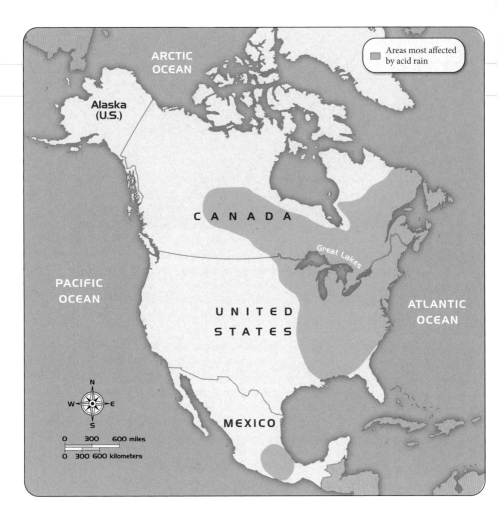

Chemical change is necessary and useful in our lives. Since ancient times, people have experimented with the matter all around them. Using chemical change, they have created thousands of medicines and products that make our lives easier, safer, and even more beautiful. Today, chemical changes are a major part of industry and manufacturing. They are happening on a massive scale. Using chemicals and chemical changes wisely is important to protect our health and the environment.

In North America, the eastern portions of the United States and Canada are hit hardest by acid rain.

atoms—the tiniest, most basic units of an element that still have all the properties of that element

chemical compound—a substance made from two or more elements that have been chemically combined

chemical element—a substance made of just one type of atom; scientists have claimed the discovery of up to 116 elements, 94 of which can be found in nature

combustion—a fast chemical change that occurs when oxygen combines with another substance

digestion—the process by which food is chemically broken down in the mouth, stomach, and intestines so that it can be absorbed into the bloodstream

DNA—a long, spiral-shaped molecule inside the body's cells that controls which traits are passed along from parents to children, such as height and hair color

electrons—tiny particles that orbit, or go around, an atom's nucleus; an electron is much smaller than a proton or a neutron, has a negative electrical charge, and does not contribute to the weight of an atom

hazardous—dangerous, particularly when relating to poisonous substances

inorganic compounds—chemical compounds that do not contain carbon

mixture—a substance made up of two or more elements that have not chemically combined

molecule—a tiny bit of matter made up of two or more atoms

neutrons—tiny particles inside an atom's nucleus; a neutron is about the same size as a proton and has no electrical charge

nucleus—the center part of an atom, made up of protons and neutrons

organic compounds—molecules containing the element carbon that are found in all living things

protons—tiny particles inside an atom's nucleus; a proton has a positive electrical charge

▶ Most compounds, by far, contain the element carbon. Scientists know of 7 million compounds containing the element carbon. The remaining 100,000 compounds in the world don't contain carbon.

▶ Hydrogen is the most plentiful chemical element in the entire universe. The sun and many stars are made mostly of hydrogen. On Earth, chemical reactions involving hydrogen produce many useful chemical products, including ammonia and hydrogen peroxide.

▶ Chemical reactions can occur when molecules absorb light. The study of these kinds of reactions is called photochemistry. Photosynthesis is the best-known example of photochemistry.

▶ Geochemists study chemical elements and compounds in soil and rocks. Knowing about Earth's chemicals helps these scientists find oil, gas, coal, and valuable ores.

▶ Materials actually have two ignition temperatures—the temperature at which a match or other energy source can cause it to burn and the temperature at which it will combust spontaneously, or on its own. Gasoline will spontaneously combust at around 752 degrees Fahrenheit (400 degrees C). No one really knows how hot wood would have to be to burst into flames on its own.

▶ Spontaneous combustion can cause dangers at home. Piles of oily rags can just suddenly burst into flames. You don't need to light them with a match. The fire starts because of chemical changes in the pile of rags. The chemical changes create heat. The heat builds up until the rags are hot enough to burst into flames. Never leave oily rags lying around in piles.

There is more oxygen and silicon than any other elements on Earth. Silicon links with oxygen to make a chemical compound called silica. Sand on deserts or beaches is made up mainly of silica.

At the Library

Newmark, Ann. *Eyewitness: Chemistry*. New York: DK Children, 2000.
Tocci, Salvatore. *The Periodic Table*. New York: Children's Press, 2004.
Whyman, Kathryn. *Everyday Chemicals*. North Mankato, Minn.: Stargazer, 2004.

On the Web

For more information on **chemical change**, use FactHound
to track down Web sites related to this book.
　　1. Go to *www.facthound.com*
　　2. Type in a search word related to this
　　　 book or this book ID: **0756512565**
　　3. Click on the *Fetch It* button.
FactHound will find the best Web sites for you.

On the Road

Maryland Science Center
　　601 Light St.
　　Baltimore, MD 21230
　　410/685-5225
　　www.mdsci.org
　　To see exhibits about DNA
　　and other science topics

The Tech Museum of Innovation
　　201 S. Market St.
　　San Jose, CA 95113
　　408/294-TECH
　　www.thetech.org
　　To learn about chemistry's role
　　in the history of technology

Museum of Science and Industry
　　5700 S. Lake Shore Drive
　　Chicago, IL 60637-2093
　　773/684-1414
　　www.msichicago.org
　　To explore hands-on exhibits
　　about chemical change
　　and other science topics

Explore all the books in this series

Chemical Change
　　From Fireworks to Rust

Erosion
　　How Land Forms, How It Changes

Manipulating Light
　　Reflection, Refraction, and Absorption

Minerals
　　From Apatite to Zinc

Natural Resources
　　Using and Protecting Earth's Supplies

Physical Change
　　Reshaping Matter

Soil
　　Digging Into Earth's Vital Resource

Waves
　　Energy on the Move